40-6314 Collection #15
Headliners Vol. 1
Pages 30-31

40-6315 Collection #16
FrameLiners Vol. 1
Pages 30-31

40-6316 Collection #17
Granny's Doodles
Pages 32-33

40-6317 Collection #18
Poems for Posterity
Pages 34-35

40-6318 Collection #19
The Cutting Edge
Pages 36-37

40-6319 Collection #20
Noah, Moses, & Friends
Pages 38-39

Bits & Bytes
Table of Contents

Bits & Bytes
#40-6323
Published by Provo Craft, Provo, Utah
Managing Editor, Louie Crandall
Directed by Ali Johnson
Photography by Craig Young

For your convenience, Provo Craft computer numbers have been listed. Wholesale orders may be placed at the Provo Craft Warehouse, 1-800-937-7686, 285 East 900 South, Provo, Utah 84606. If you do not have a wholesale account, you may order retail from the Provo Craft Shipping Department, 1-800-563-8679, 295 West Center Street, Provo, Utah 84601. The Provo Craft products and other craft items used in this book are available at Robert's retail stores (located in Utah and Idaho) and other fine craft stores.

ISBN 1-58050-119-2

Provo Craft will make every effort to maintain an inventory of those products shown in this book; however, we cannot guarantee that they will be available for the sales life of the book.

A Child's World by Marie Cole

Greeting Card (A.)

Supplies:

White Card Stock
Coordinating Scrapbook Paper
Scissors
Adhesive
Black Permanent Marker
Embellishments (ribbon, buttons, etc.)

Sample Supplies:

40-0114 "That's My Baby" Scrap Pad Paper
4 - 1/2" Yellow Buttons
1/8" Blue Ribbon (6")

1. Choose your font and images and size to fit your card.
2. Print the images on white card stock.
3. Print the poem on scrapbook paper, leaving space for the images.
4. Carefully cut out the images.
5. Adhere a piece of scrapbook paper to the outside of the card (white card stock) and fold in half.
6. Decorate the front of the card with scrapbook paper.
7. Adhere the poem and images to the center of the card.
8. Use a black permanent marker to draw trails behind the butterfly and bee.
9. Embellish the front of the card with ribbon and buttons.

Iron-On Transfer Designs (B.)

Supplies:

Doily or T-Shirt
Xerox Iron-On Transfer Sheet
Scissors

1. Choose your images and size to fit your doily or shirt.
2. Print the images on iron-on transfer paper. (Make sure you indicate on your printer that it is a transfer printed backwards.)
3. Cut around the images and position them on the doily or shirt.
4. Following the instructions on the packaging, iron the images onto the doily or shirt.

Frame (C.)

Supplies:

Unpainted Wood Frame
White Paper
Scrapbook Paper
Scissors
Mod Podge
Black Permanent Marker
White Acrylic Paint

Sample Supplies:

11-2632 8" x 8" Square Frame
40-0114 "That's My Baby" Scrap Pad Paper

1. Choose your font and images.
2. Size the images and poem to fit the frame.
3. Print the poem and images on white paper.
4. Carefully cut out the images.
5. Following the instructions on the bottle, Mod Podge scrapbook paper to the front of the frame.
6. Mod Podge the images to the front of the frame.
7. Mod Podge the entire front of the frame for a finish.
8. Using white acrylic paint, paint the edge of the frame.
9. Place the poem in the opening.

Lampshade (D.)

Supplies:

Lampshade
Coordinating Scrapbook Paper
Scissors
Embellishments (ribbon, buttons, etc.)
Hole Punch
Mod Podge
White Card Stock
Black Permanent Marker
Acrylic Paint
Glue

Sample Supplies:

40-0114 "That's My Baby" Scrap Pad Paper
Lampshade (9" wide x 7" high x 4" across top)
5 - 1/2" Pink Buttons
3/8" Mint Green Satin Ribbon (1 yard)
Yellow and White Acrylic Paint

1. Size the images and print on white card stock.
2. Carefully cut out the images.
3. Paint the lampshade, including the top and bottom rims and let dry.
4. Cut five strips of scrapbook paper to go around the lampshade. (The top corners should connect, making triangles in between the strips of paper.)
5. Following the instructions on the bottle, Mod Podge the papers to the lampshade. Let dry.
6. Mod Podge the images onto the papers and the lampshade.
7. Use a black permanent marker to make trails behind the butterflies and bees.
8. Mod Podge the entire lampshade to give it a finish. Let dry.
9. Glue embellishments around the top of the lampshade.
10. Punch holes around the bottom of the lampshade, alternating 1/2" and 1/4" apart.
11. Thread ribbon through the holes and tie in a bow.

B.
A.
B.
Childhood is filled with Hopes and Dreams,
Sprinkled with Fairy Dust and Happily Ever Afters.
C.
BELIEVE
In Your Dreams and Happily Ever Afters
D.

This 'n That by Annette Ward

Basketball Scrapbook Page (A.)

Supplies:

White Paper
Colored Paper
White Card Stock
Scissors
Glue

1. Print the images on white paper.
2. Cut, leaving a white border, and mount the images on colored paper.
3. Mount the photos on colored paper.
4. Add colored paper strips to the top and bottom of white card stock.
5. Glue the images and photos in place.
6. Add journaling.

Halloween Box (B.)

Supplies:

Small Box with Handle
White Card Stock
Scissors
Decorative Edged Scissors
Orange Paper
Thin Wire
Black Ribbon

1. Print the images on white card stock.
2. Cut out the images, leaving a white border.
3. Using decorative scissors, cut a piece of orange paper to fit the front of the box and glue in place.
4. Glue the witch and the cat to the front of the box.
5. Cut a piece of thin wire and attach one end with tape to the back side of the bat. Wrap the remaining wire around the handle of the box and curl the remaining end of the wire.
6. Fill the box with your favorite treat. Tie a black bow on the handle.

Santa Tag and Border on Gift Bag (C.)

Supplies:

White Paper
Colored Card Stock
Scissors
Decorative Edged Scissors
Gift Bag
Colored Markers
Ribbon

1. Print the tag and border on white paper.
2. Cut out the images, leaving a white border.
3. Mount the tag on colored card stock.
4. Cut around the edge of the tag with decorative edged scissors.
5. Write in the information on the tag and attach to the gift.
6. Glue the Santa border about 1/2" from the bottom of the bag. Either wrap the border all around the bag or just wrap a small amount around each side.
7. Using markers, add dots and stripes on the bag. Tie a bow on the handle.

Candy Wrapper (D.)

Supplies:

White Paper
Decorative Edged Scissors
Scissors
Glue
Double Stick Tape
Colored Marker

1. Print the "cupcake" and "happy birthday" images on white paper.
2. Pencil a 6 1/2" x 5" rectangle centered around the image. (You may need to adjust the size depending on the size of your candy.)
3. Using decorative edged scissors, cut on the sides of the rectangle over the pencil lines. Straight cut on the top and bottom edges.
4. Glue the rectangle on colored background paper.
5. Straight cut the sides of the background paper, leaving a 1/4" border.
6. Using a colored marker, add swirls and dots on the entire wrapper.
7. Wrap around your candy and adjust the length if needed. Using double stick tape, tape the wrapper closed.

Baby Card (E.)

Supplies:

White Card Stock
Scissors
X-acto Knife
Colored Markers
Ribbon

1. Print the image on white card stock. (Make sure to leave enough room around the image to make the card.)
2. Cut a 6 1/4" length x 4 1/2" width rectangle around the image. Lightly pencil a line through the middle of the card. (This is where the card will fold.) Do not fold the card yet!
3. Using an X-acto knife, cut around the top part of the baby to the pencil line. Fold the card, making the baby "pop out".
4. With markers, add trim lines to the outside edge of the card. Add random dots on the front of the card.
5. Tie a small bow and glue in place on the card.
6. You can use this card for a baby announcement, baby shower invitation or gift tag.

A.
basketball
B.
C.
merry christmas
D.
birthday
E.
BABY

Color Me Kids by Amy Dott

Iron-On Transfer Projects (A.)

Create great personalized gifts for your kids, friends, teachers or even a new bride and groom. You can make transfers to use on t-shirts, aprons, bags and even quilt squares.

Supplies:

Transfer Item (t-shirt, bag, apron, etc.)
Xerox Iron-On Transfer Paper

1. Select the images you want to transfer. Enlarge to fit the item you are using. Personalize by adding names.
2. Print the images on transfer paper. (Make sure you indicate on your printer that it is a transfer printed backwards.)
3. Following the directions on the packaging, iron the images onto the item you are using.

Cards (B.)

Create birth announcements, invitations, thank you cards, holiday and moving cards using the images on this CD. Personalizing your creations is easy when you use the faces and full body figures to match your family. Give your creations an extra touch by adding the names next to the faces or bodies. The art is so simple and fun, people will think you drew your own cards.

Supplies:

Card Stock
Scissors
Vellum (optional)
Ribbon (optional)
Hole punch (optional)

1. Choose a font and images for your card.
2. Enlarge or reduce the image to fit your card.
3. Print the images and text on card stock or vellum.
4. Cut the card stock around the text and images.
5. Attach vellum to card stock with ribbon.

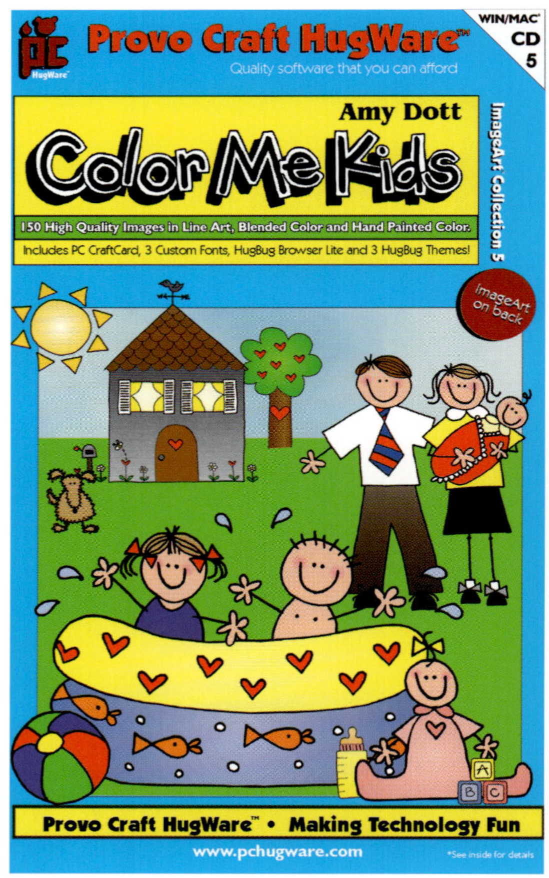

40-6303

Labels (C.)

Add a personal touch to all your letters by creating your own return address labels. Select the faces to match the members of your family and add your name and address. The birthday and holiday images make gift labeling a snap.

Supplies:

White Address Labels (any size)

1. Choose your font and images.
2. Type the text and position the images.
3. Enlarge or reduce the text and images to fit the label.
4. Print on label sheets.

A.
WE LOVE MOM!
Dad
Mom
Sally
Alex
B.
It's my 4th Birthday and I want you to come...
Friday, July 10th 3:00 p.m.
Come for cake, ice cream and lots of fun.
Love, Lindsey
A.
SCHOOL
Student of the Month
BILLY
A.
Eliza's Ballet Bag
B.
It's a Party for...
JAYSON!
C.
Happy Birthday Todd
From Zack
B.
We've Moved!
On the Road to Texas

Simple Folk by Jill Webster

Plant Stakes (A.)

Supplies:

- Dowel (any width and length desired)
- Scissors
- White Card Stock
- Hot Glue

1. Choose your image and enlarge to size desired.
2. Print image on white card stock.
3. Cut out the image.
4. Using hot glue, glue the image to a dowel.

Calendar (B.)

Supplies:

- White Glue
- Scissors
- Card Stock
- Small Paper Calendar

1. Choose and print your image, glue to card stock.
2. Glue calendar to card stock, then cut around calendar and card image. Glue magnet to back.

Note Pad in Pail (C.)

Supplies:

- White Paper
- Scissors
- Pail (or other container)
- Glue

Sample Supplies:

- 11-2384 Medium Rectangle Pail with Handle

1. Choose a background design.
2. Print on white paper and cover the pail.
3. Choose an image for the front of the pail and enlarge.
4. Print on white paper, cut and adhere to the front of the pail.
5. Choose a border or images for the paper.
6. Position and print several copies.
7. Cut out the paper and mount the top part of the sheets together.

Get Framed by Fayette Terlouw (see following page)

Mummy and Ghost Gift Tags (A.)

Supplies:

- Black and White Index Papers
- Scissors
- Small Brown Gift Bag
- Black Raffia
- Black and Orange Tissue Paper

1. Open "Candy Corn Frame.wmf" for each gift tag.
2. Open "Spider.wmf" and adjust to desired size.
3. Open the "Mummy Topper.wmf" and "Ghost Topper.wmf". Center each topper over a frame. Make sure that their hands are over the front of the sign.
4. Open "Mummy Feet.wmf" and "Ghost Feet.wmf" and center them on the bottom of the signs. The mummy's feet should be over the sign. The ghost's body should be placed behind the frame.
5. Print on index paper.
6. You may have to use a gray colored pencil and fill in any white spaces left between the "Mummy Topper.wmf" and the "Spooky Frame.wmf".
7. Trim around the gift tags and spiders, leaving a small white border on all sides.
8. Glue the gift tags and spiders to black index paper. Cut out again, leaving approximately 1/8" of black showing on all sides.
9. Use a black marker to draw a spider web on one lower corner of the bag.
10. Place the tissue paper and your treat inside the bag. Tie a raffia bow on the handle. Glue, tie or tape the gift tags to the raffia. Tie one piece of black raffia off of the other side of the handle. Glue the spider to the other end of the raffia and adhere over the spider web.

"That's Our Boy" Scrapbook Page (B.)

Supplies:

- 12" x 12" Background Paper
- Glue
- Yellow and White Index Paper
- Scissors
- Scallop Edged Scissors

Sample Supplies:

- 42-5156 12" x 12" "Zany Zoo Sky" Paper

1. Open "Heart Check Frame.wmf" and size to fit your photo.
2. Open "Baby Topper.wmf" and center over the top edge of the frame. Place "Baby Face 4.wmf" in the center of the baby's face.
3. Open "Ducks.wmf" and size to desired size for your page. I mirrored one set of ducks to balance the page.
4. Print out on index paper.
5. Using the "PC Little Squiggles" font, type your headline for the page. I used 65 point font size. Print on index paper.
6. Using scallop edged scissors, cut around the frame. Cut around the baby, leaving a small white border on all sides. Cut out the ducks.
7. Cut out the center of the frame and line with a 1/4" yellow matte around the inside.
8. Cut the letters into 3/4" blocks and glue each one to a 1 1/8" yellow block.
9. Glue all of the pieces in place as shown in the photo.
10. Mount the ducks to the page using photo mount to give it a 3-D appearance.

"You're Beary Special" Greeting Card (C.)

Supplies:

- White Index Paper
- Dotted Vellum Paper
- Background Paper
- Glue
- Scissors
- Scallop Edged Scissors

Sample Supplies:

- 42-6311 8 1/2" x 11" Pomegranate "Spatter Dot" Paper

1. Open "Heart Check Frame.wmf" and adjust to desired size.
2. Open "Bear & Hearts.wmf" and center over the bottom inside edge of the frame. Print on white index paper.
3. Type the text using the "Little Squiggles" font, 60 point size. Print on the Pomegranate paper.
4. Cut the edges and inside of the frame out with scallop edged scissors.
5. Cut the vellum to fit behind the opening in the frame and glue in place.
6. Glue the Pomegranate paper inside the card so that the text is centered in the opening of the frame.

Spooky Poster (D.)

Supplies:

- Black and White Index Paper
- Decorative Edged Scissors

1. Open "Spooky Frame.wmf" and enlarge to approximately 6 3/4" high.
2. Open "Dracula Topper.wmf" and "Witch Topper.wmf" and place them at the top of the sign with their hands "holding" the sign.
3. Use the "PC Geo Angles" font to add your text.
4. Print onto white paper.
5. Trim around Dracula and the Witch leaving a small white border on all sides. Cut along the sign using decorative edged scissors. (I used large zig zag scissors.)
6. Glue to a piece of black index paper.

Continued on following page.

A.
B.
C.
D.
E.
F.
THAT'S OUR BOY
Jake 4 Months
THE MONSTER MASH!
GRANDPA'S PLACE
A.
F.

Pilgrim Place Marker (E.)

Supplies:

- White Index Paper
- X-acto Knife

1. Open "Check Frame.wmf" and shrink it to the desired size. Place the frame near the bottom edge of the paper on your screen.
2. Open "Pilgrim Topper.wmf" and center him on the top edge of the frame. Make sure that his hands are properly placed, overlapping the frame.
3. Open "Scarecrow Feet.wmf" and center them on the bottom edge of the frame. The soles of his shoes should be slightly below the edge of the frame.
4. Use "PC RoundAbout" font and type your text, centered inside of the opening on the frame. (I used a 48 point size font.)
5. Print your project onto index paper.
6. Use an X-acto knife to cut around the Pilgrim's hands, collar and head. It's easier if you leave a small white margin all around where you're cutting, rather than trying to cut right on the black line. Lightly score your paper where you want it to fold.
7. Trim the excess paper from the edges and fold in half.

"Hang in There" Kitty Magnet (F.)

Supplies:

- White and Medium Blue Index Paper
- Scissors
- Magnetic Strip
- Laminating Paper
- Glue

1. Open "Hearts String Line.wmf" and size it to approximately 4 1/2" wide.
2. Open "Cat Topper.wmf" and center it over the three large red hearts on the border. (I cut off the last small yellow heart for this project.)
3. Open "Cat Feet.wmf" and center on the bottom edge of the border.
4. Print onto white index paper. Cut out leaving a small white border all the way around. On the right side of the border (facing project) cut the small yellow heart and some string off so that the red hearts are in the same distance from each side.
5. Glue the cat to the blue index paper. Laminate and attach a magnetic strip to the back of the project.

Turkey Treat Holder (G.)

Supplies:

- White Index Paper
- Brown Paper Bag
- Scissors
- Glue
- X-acto Knife
- Circle Template
- Cellophane Raffia

1. Open "Give Thanks.wmf". Size the give thanks sign so that it measures approximately 3 3/4" wide. Paste another "Give Thanks.wmf" directly beside the first one you opened.
2. Open "Turkey Topper.wmf" and center it over one of the Give Thanks signs. Make sure that his wings overlap onto the sign and that the top line of the sign and bottom line of the turkey line up correctly.
3. Open "Turkey Feet.wmf" and center them on the bottom edge of the sign.
4. Print this project out on white index paper. Trim around this project leaving a small white border on all sides.
5. I made a small "insert" cup out of a brown paper bag to go inside my turkey. If you prefer, you can just use a paper or plastic nut cup to go inside. To make the paper insert, trace around a 2 1/4" circle on a brown paper bag. Lightly score along this line. Cut small "V"s out all around the border of the circle making sure that you don't cut inside your scored line. Fold up along the scored line. Cut a strip of brown paper bag 1 1/2" high by approximately 8 1/2" wide. Glue this strip to the circle. Position the Turkey Treat Holder around the insert and glue in place. Fill a small cellophane bag with goodies, tie with raffia and place inside the insert.

40-6306

Cook-ie Crumbs by Kristin Cook

Camp Awards and Camp Sign (A.)

Supplies:
- 8 1/2" x 11" White Card Stock
- Scrapbook Paper
- Scissors
- Double Stick Tape or Glue
- Hole Punch
- Raffia

Sample Supplies:
- 42-5249 12" x 12" "Field of Flowers" Paper
- 42-5239 12" x 12" "Basket Weaving" Paper

1. Choose your font and images and size to fit your paper.
2. Print on white card stock.
3. Mount on 12" x 12" scrapbook paper, cut to make an even border around the white card stock.
4. Punch two holes, one inch apart, in the top of the sign.
5. Thread raffia through the holes and tie in a bow.

T-Shirt (B.)

Supplies:
- White T-Shirt
- Xerox Iron-On Transfer Paper
- Scissors

1. Choose your font and image and size to fit your shirt.
2. Print on transfer paper. (Make sure you indicate on your printer that it is a transfer printed backwards.)
3. Cut around the image.
4. Following the instructions on the packaging, iron the image onto the shirt.

Camp Journal (C.)

Supplies:
- 2 Sheets Corrugated Paper
- Coordinating Scrapbook Paper
- Plain Writing Paper (for inside)
- Jute Rope (2 pieces cut 12" long)
- Scissors
- Hole Punch
- Glue or Double Stick Tape
- White Card Stock
- Photo

Sample Supplies:
- 40-0106 "Let's Party" Scrap Pad Paper

1. Choose your font and images.
2. Size the images to fit on the cover of your journal.
3. Print the images on white card stock.
4. Cut out the images.
5. Adhere scrapbook paper to the cover.
6. Adhere the images to the scrapbook paper on the cover.
7. If desired, add a photo to the cover.
8. Using a hole punch, punch two sets of holes 1 3/4" from the top and bottom of the journal. Punch holes in the front and back covers and the writing paper.
9. To hold the journal together, thread jute thread through the holes and tie in knots.

Bug Jar (D.)

Supplies:
- Glass Jar
- Natural Raffia
- Scissors
- Clear Glue
- White Card Stock
- Hole Punch

1. Wrap raffia around the neck of the jar and tie in a bow.
2. Choose your font and images and size to fit the jar.
3. Print the words and images on white card stock.
4. Cut out the images and glue to the front of the jar.
5. Attach "Today's Catch" to the raffia using a hole punch.

Note: Instructions for the Rustic Woodland Birdhouse in the photo can be found in the book Rustic Retreat (40-6224) by Christine Sax.

40-6307

A.
Welcome
To
Camp Mia Shalom
C.
(picture)
My
Camp
Journal
"Eat all the bugs you want."
B.
A.
Camp Award
for the
Cleanest
Camp Site
WELCOME
Todays
Catch
BUG JAR
D.

Never A Dull Moment by Cara Bradshaw

Sailor Hat (A.)

Supplies:

- White Sailor Hat
- Scissors
- 6 - 1/2" Buttons
- Hot Glue
- Pin Clasp
- Laminating
- White Card Stock
- Permanent Marker

1. Clip the boat from the boat shirt and size (2" x 2").
2. Print the boat on card stock.
3. Cut out the boat and laminate.
4. Glue the pin clasp to the back of the boat.
5. Evenly sew or glue buttons around the band of the hat.
6. Using a permanent marker, write on the edge of the hat: "Whatever floats your boat."
7. Pin the boat below the words.

Tin Lunch Pail Magnet Dolls (B.)

Supplies:

- Small White Tin Pail
- Stencils
- Old Toothbrush or Stiff Paintbrush to make paint spatters
- Acrylic Paint
- Paintbrushes
- Magnetic Sheets for your printer (12 millimeter matte)
- Scissors
- Clear Acrylic Finishing Spray

Sample Supplies:

- 20-7013 Rectangle Lunch Box
- Red, Yellow & Blue Acrylic Paint
- Plaid and Star Stencils

1. Enlarge the little boy, little girl and clothes, keeping in mind the size of your pail and making sure the clothes fit the dolls.
2. Print the images on magnetic sheets.
3. Cut out all of the images.
4. Decorate the pail as desired using acrylic paint and stencils.
5. To seal the paint, spray the pail with clear acrylic finishing spray.
6. When not in use, store the dolls and clothes inside the pail.

Boy and Girl T-Shirt (C.)

Supplies:

- White T-Shirt
- Xerox Iron-On Transfer Paper
- 1/8" Ribbon (6")
- Needle and Thread

1. Enlarge the little boy and little girl with clothes to fit your shirt.
2. Print the images on iron-on transfer paper. (Make sure you indicate on your printer that it is a transfer printed backwards.)
3. Following the directions on the packaging, iron the images onto the shirt.
4. Tie a bow with the ribbon and sew onto the front collar of the shirt.

Boy and Girl Card (D.)

Supplies:

- Blank White Card or Card Stock
- Coordinating Scrapbook Paper
- Double Stick Tape
- Glue
- Scissors
- Embellishments (ribbon, buttons, etc.)

Sample Supplies:

- 40-0112 "Spring Break" Scrap Pad
- 1/8" Red Ribbon (6")
- 4 - 1/8" Red Buttons

1. Fold the card or card stock in half.
2. Cover the outside of the card with scrapbook paper.
3. Cut two pieces of coordinating scrapbook paper and adhere to the cover with double stick tape.
4. Dress the girl and boy in the desired clothing and choose any other images desired.
5. Print the images on white card stock.
6. Cut the images to fit the card and adhere to the front cover with double stick tape.
7. Embellish the front cover of the card.

40-6308

A.
... Whatever Float Your Boat ...
B.
Summertime is: Children ~ laughter ~ Sunshine ~ ice cream ~ Swimming hole ~ Sandcastle ~ lemon
Picnic ~ Sailboats ~ Watermellon
C.
D.

Family Frenzy by Leere' Aldrich

3-D Picture Frames (A.)

Supplies:

- Acrylic Photo Frame
- Sticker Paper
- Sticky Back Craft Foam
- Ribbons, sequins, buttons, etc.
- Scissors
- Glue

1. Print the images and background on sticker paper.
2. Carefully cut out the images following the outline of the artwork.
3. Peel the sticker back off of the sticker paper and attach the image to the craft foam. Note: It is very important to cut out your image BEFORE adhering it to the foam.
4. Cut around your image again. You can either cut the foam right on the outline of the image or leave a 1/8" to 1/4" border around the image.
5. Repeat step four until you have the desired depth for the 3-D effect.
6. Cut out the frame or background sticker paper and attach to the frame. (A layer of craft foam can be added between the frame and background paper if desired.)
7. Attach the 3-D image to the frame by removing the sticky back on the foam. (If part of the image hangs over the edge of the frame you will need to cover the sticky back with a piece of paper cut to size.
8. Embellish the frame and or the 3-D image with ribbons, sequins, etc.

Personalized Calendar Mouse Pads (B.)

Have a calendar handy right under your mouse! For a refreshing change, make one for each month or season. These make great gifts! Leave out the calendar and make a brag mouse pad for Grandma or Daddy's office.

Supplies:

- Inexpensive Mouse Pad
- Photo Paper for your printer
- Scanned in or Digital Photos
- Scissors
- Xyron Machine

1. Print the images, calendar and photos on photo paper for your printer.
2. Cut out the photo paper using the mouse pad as a guide.
3. Run the precut photo paper through a Xyron machine to make the back sticky and attach to a mouse pad.

Journal (C.)

Supplies:

- Scanned in, digital or regular photos
- Photo Paper for your printer
- Notebook with fabric edge
- Xyron Machine
- Frog Closure
- Ribbon
- Buttons, Sequins, etc.
- Glue
- Scissors

1. Print the images and photos on photo paper for your printer.
2. Cut out the photo paper to fit the cover of the notebook.
3. Run the precut photo paper through a Xyron machine to laminate.
4. Attach the laminated photo paper to the front of the notebook.
5. Glue a piece of ribbon to the back of the notebook. Cut the ribbon long enough to bring it around to the front. Glue another short piece of ribbon to the front just above the piece that comes around from the back.
6. Glue a frog closure to the two pieces of ribbon.
7. Embellish the notebook with sequins, buttons, etc.

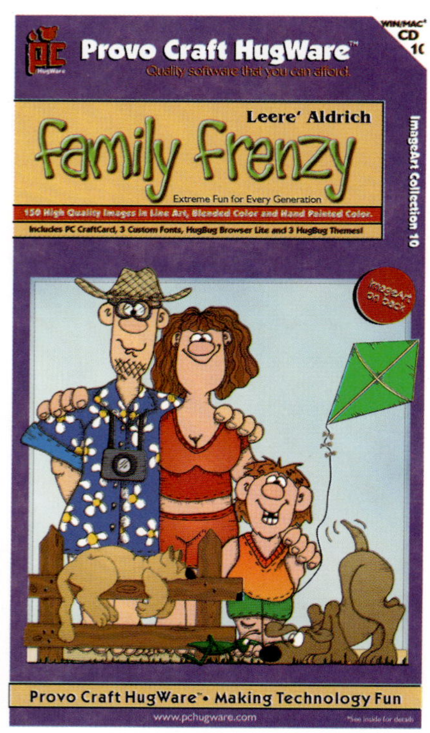

40-6309

B.
A.
B.
C.
A.
C.
A.

It's a Wonderful Life by Julie Young

Gift Tags (A)

Supplies:
- White Paper or Card Stock
- Colored Card Stock
- Scissors
- Hole Punch
- Ribbon

1. Choose your font and images and design your gift tag.
2. Print your gift tag on white paper or card stock.
3. Cut out the tag.
4. If desired, mount the tag on colored card stock.
5. Punch a hole in the tag and attach to the gift using ribbon.

40-6310

Plant Pick (B.)

Supplies:
- Flexi-Foam™
- Dowel
- White Glue
- Scissors

1. Choose image, adjust it to your chosen size, and print.
2. Cut around edge of image.
3. Mount image with glue onto white Flexi-Foam™.
4. Cut around image, leaving a white border of foam.
5. Glue dowel onto back.
6. Insert into plant!

Don't Forget Card (C.)

Supplies:
- Button
- Ribbon
- Plaid Paper
- Glue
- Hole punch

1. Print hand and tag on white card stock.
2. Glue on plaid paper for sleeve material.
3. Attach tag to finger using ribbon through a punched hole.
4. Glue button on at wrist.
5. Write message on back or inside as desired.

A.
Lovie Dovie
A.
here's my heart
A.
A STAR is born
DAD... don't forget
C.
how much I love you!
B.
for my best BUD
A.

Borders, Corners & More by Kathy Griffiths

Scrapbook Page (A.)

Supplies:
- White Paper
- Scissors
- 2 Coordinating Scrapbook Papers
- Solid Color Card Stock
- Photos
- Acid Free Adhesive

Sample Supplies:
- 42-5262 12" x 12" Stonewashed Denim "Basic Check" Paper
- 42-5257 12" x 12" Stonewashed Denim "Spatter Dot" Paper

1. Choose the corners and images that you would like to use on your scrapbook page and print on white paper.
2. Carefully cut out the images.
3. Double mat your photos using scrapbook paper and solid color card stock and adhere to the scrapbook page.
4. Adhere the corner images to the corners of the photos and mats.
5. Adhere any images and lettering.

Certificate (B.)

Supplies:
- Card Stock
- Colored Card Stock
- Photo Mounting Squares
- Decorative Edged Scissors

1. Create a certificate using HugWare fonts, corners and images.
2. Print on white card stock or neutral color.
3. Cut the edge of the certificate using decorative edged scissors.
4. Mount the certificate on colored card stock, matching the colors used on the certificate.

Postcard (C.)

Supplies:
- Card Stock

1. Design a postcard using HugWare images.
2. Print the postcard on card stock.
3. Write a note on the front and adhere a photo on the back.
4. Address the postcard and don't forget the stamp.

School Journal (D.)

Supplies:
- 2 Sheets Corrugated Paper
- Card Stock
- 50 Sheets Paper
- Jute
- Paper Punch
- Printed Paper
- Decorative Edged Scissors
- Photo Mounting Squares
- Ribbon

1. Cut a rectangle, slightly larger than your photo, in the center of the corrugated paper for the cover.
2. Frame your photo with card stock and place behind the opening on the cover.
3. Print HugWare corner images on card stock. Cut images and adhere to the journal cover.
4. Design the journal pages using images and numbers. Print on plain paper.
5. Punch two sets of holes on the left side of the corrugated papers and the plain paper approximately 1 1/2" apart.
6. Thread ribbon through the holes to bind the journal together and tie into bows.
7. Print an apple image with the grade number on it and tie it to the journal using jute.
8. Print and adhere a small tag for the cover that says, "My School Journal".
9. Using decorative edged scissors, cut printed paper for a border around the photo.

Pencil Topper (E.)

Supplies:
- White Card Stock
- Scissors
- Hot Glue/Glue Gun
- Pencil

1. If desired, type text on two mirror image icons. Print on white card stock.
2. Cut the icons around the borders.
3. Using hot glue, attach the icons to the end of a pencil.

Gift Card (F.)

Supplies:
- White Card Stock
- Scissors

1. Choose a border for the top and bottom of your card.
2. Type "To" and "From" in the center of the card.
3. Print the card on white card stock.
4. Cut out the card.
5. Write in the names and attach to a gift.

A.
Wyatt
B.
Sage Creek Elementary School
certifies that
McKenzie Neff
has successfully completed first grade
May 26, 2000
(Teacher)
(Principal)
C.
D.
Day 1
E.
this Book
Belongs To:
McKenzie
F.
To: Mrs. Maltin
My School Journal
gift certificate
to: My Sweetheart
from: Your Hubby
good for: Dinners on Friday
issued by: Mark
date: 6-1-00
expires: Never

Peeking Thru the Garden Gate by Debbie Lewis & Lorie Lakey

Window Hanging (A.)

Supplies:
- White Paper
- Ribbon
- Scissors
- Laminate
- Hole Punch

1. Enlarge the images to the size desired.
2. Print the images on white paper.
3. Cut out the images using small scissors to cut around the details.
4. Adhere all of the images together except the watering can.
5. Laminate all of the images.
6. Cut around the images.
7. Using a hole punch, make two holes in the top of the window and one hole in the watering can.
8. Tie the watering can to the window with ribbon.
9. Use the ribbon to hang the window.

Vegetable Magnets (B.)

Supplies:
- White Card Stock
- Laminate
- Scissors
- Magnets
- Hot Glue

1. Enlarge the items to the size desired.
2. Print on white card stock.
3. Cut out the images using small scissors to cut around the details.
4. Laminate the images.
5. Cut around the images.
6. Glue a magnet to the back of each image.

T-Shirt (C.)

Supplies:
- White T-Shirt
- Xerox Iron-On Transfer Paper

5. Choose your font and image and size to fit your shirt.
6. Print on transfer paper. (Make sure you indicate on your printer that it is a transfer printed backwards.)
7. Cut around the image.
8. Following the instructions on the packaging, iron the image onto the shirt.

Jar of Carrots (D.)

Supplies:
- Large Glass Jar
- White Paper
- Corrugated Paper
- Coordinating Scrapbook Paper
- Double Stick Tape
- Raffia
- Laminate
- Scissors
- Hole Punch
- Fabric
- Cotton

Sample Supplies:
- 42-6283 8 1/2" x 11" Buttercream Wavy Plaid Paper
- 42-6258 8 1/2" x 11" Field of Flowers Paper

1. Size and print the images on white paper.
2. Cut out the images.
3. .Laminate all the images except the garden seeds packet.
4. Cut around the laminated images.
5. Using double stick tape, wrap coordinating scrapbook paper strips around the jar.
6. Wrap a strip of corrugated paper around the jar, on top of the scrapbook paper.
7. Punch two holes, using a hole punch, in the front of the center laminated image.
8. Tie the image to the jar by threading raffia through the holes and wrapping around the jar and tying in a knot.
9. Make a card to attach by cutting and folding scrapbook paper in half.
10. Adhere the garden seeds packet image to the front of the card.
11. Make a hole in the upper left corner of the card and the handles of the tools.
12. Tie the card and tools to the neck of the jar with raffia.
13. Tie a piece of fabric filled with cotton to the lid with raffia.

Continued on following page...

Peeking Thru the Garden Gate by Debbie Lewis & Lorie Lakey, cont.

Garden Seed Gift Packet (E.)

Supplies:

- 8 1/2" x 11" Tan Card Stock
- Cream Card Stock
- 3 1/2" x 8 1/2" Cardboard
- Hole Punch
- Background Paper
- 1/8" Ribbon
- 2" x 11" Corrugated Paper
- French Wired Ribbon

Sample Supplies:

- 42-6258 8 1/2" x 11" "Field of Flowers" Paper
- 42-6284 8 1/2" x 11" Buttercream "Basic Check" Paper

1. Print the text and images onto the inside side panels on tan card stock.
2. Print five seed packet covers onto cream card stock.
3. Following the seed packet pattern, fold and glue coordinating background paper into seed packets, leaving one end open for seeds.
4. Glue the seed packet covers onto the seed packets.
5. Fill the packets with the appropriate seeds and glue shut.
6. Arrange the packets vertically onto a strip of cardboard. Staple the top of the seed packets in place starting at the bottom then laying the next seed packet in place on top of the bottom seed packet. Staple all of the packets except the top packet. Using a 1/8" - 3/16" hole punch, punch two small holes in the top of the seed packet, the cardboard and card stock. Using a 1/8" ribbon, tie a small bow to secure the cardboard strip to the tan card stock.
7. To decorate the outside of the packet, layer 11" long strips of coordinating paper to the center of the card stock. Glue each strip with about 1/2" of paper on either side. Glue the corrugated paper last.
8. Fold the packet over the center, covering the seeds.
9. Glue ribbon to the outside of the packet to tie closed.

Ribbon Hanging (F.)

Supplies:

- Satin Wire Edged Ribbon
- White Card Stock
- Glue
- Scissors
- Hole Punch

1. Size and print the images on white card stock.
2. Cut out the images.
3. Adhere the images to the ribbon.
4. Punch two holes in the ribbon image and tie a bow.

Large Envelope (G.)

Supplies:

- Coordinating Scrapbook Paper
- White Card Stock
- Colored Card Stock
- Wire Edged Ribbon
- Scissors
- Double Stick Tape
- Hole Punch

Sample Supplies

- 42-6281 8 1/2" x 11" Buttercream Suede Paper
- 42-6283 8 1/2" x 11" Buttercream Wavy Plaid
- 42-5256 12" x 12" Buttercream Basic Check

1. Choose an image, size and print on white card stock.
2. Cut out the image using small scissors to cut around the details.
3. Print the garden seeds packet on colored card stock.
4. .Cut and fold the colored card stock to form a card.
5. Fold a 12" x 12" piece of scrapbook paper to form an envelope. Fold the inside edges in toward the center.
6. Decorate the edge of the envelope with coordinating strips of scrapbook paper.
7. Punch a hole in the vegetable image and tie to the envelope with ribbon.
8. Tuck the garden seed packet card under the ribbon.

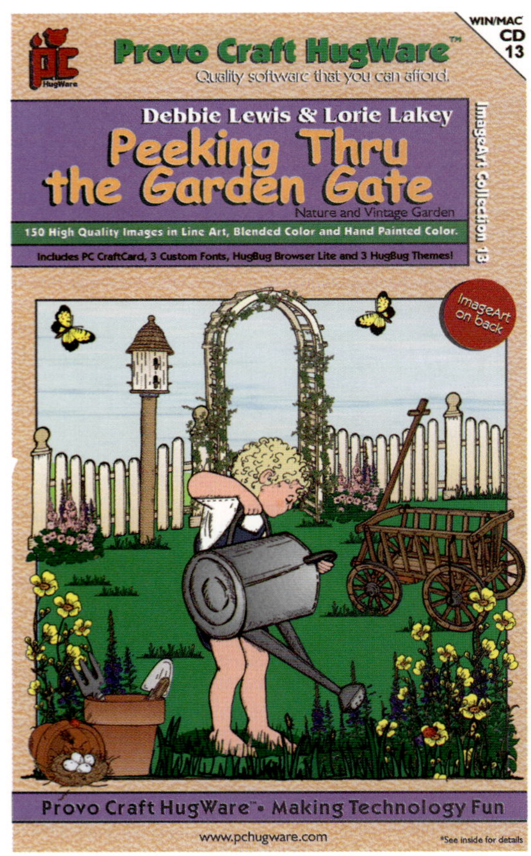

40-6312

Little Images by Rebecca Carter

Simple Things (A.)

Supplies:

- 8" x 10" Frame
- Tan Card Stock
- Scissors
- Cream Card Stock

1. Enlarge the photo to approximately 5 1/4" x 7 1/4"
2. Print the photo and mount it on cream card stock leaving a 1/8" border.
3. Double mount the photo on tan card stock leaving a 1/8" border.
4. Print the saying on the bottom on cream card stock, keeping in mind the 8" x 10" measurement.
5. Adhere the photo to the upper area of the printed card stock.
6. Place into a frame.

Bookmark (B.)

Supplies:

- Green Card Stock
- Cream Card Stock
- Tan Card Stock
- Scissors
- Paper Punch
- Ribbon
- Laminate

1. Choose a photo and reduce to approximately 1 1/2" x 3".
2. Print the photo and cut.
3. Mount the photo on tan card stock, leaving a 1/8" border.
4. Print the phrase to fit the bookmark on cream card stock.
5. Cut the cream card stock to appropriate size.
6. Mount the cream card stock on green card stock leaving a 1/4" border.
7. Mount the photo to the bookmark approximately 1 1/4" from the top.
8. Laminate the bookmark and cut around the edge.
9. Punch two holes at the top and tie the ribbon.

School Book Cover (C.)

This project can be made as a laminate and adhered to the front of a book or slid into a sleeve of a binder.

Supplies:

- Card Stock
- Scissors
- Photo Corners
- Laminate

1. Size the photo and print.
2. Trim the photo and adhere to card stock, leaving a 1/8" border.
3. Adhere photo corners to the photo.
4. Print the lettering on card stock, leaving a space for the photo.
5. Adhere the mounted photo to the card stock.
6. Laminate or slide into a binder sleeve.

Remember All The Little Things (D.)

Supplies:

- 6 1/2" x 14 1/2" Frame
- Sage Green Paper
- White Card Stock
- Scissors
- Deckle Edged Scissors

1. Reduce the selected photos to approximately 3" x 2".
2. Print and trim the photos. Mount the photos onto white card stock and trim with deckle edged scissors, leaving a 1/4" border.
3. Print the saying along the bottom section on sage green paper keeping in mind the frame size.
4. Adhere the photos in the top 2/3 of the sage green paper, evenly spaced.
5. Insert into the frame.

Continued on following page...

A.
Embrace the beauty of silent moments and simple things.
B.
In Books
C.
Ms. Miller's
Book of Grades
A good book is a good friend.
D.
emember all the little things
E.
Mitchell
Summer 1999
F.
Congratulations!

Mini Scrapbook Cover (E.)

Note: Some photo albums are sealed and need to be cut open to remove inner back and covers. Carefully cut from the inside of the cover next to the binding. Don't cut through both layers of the plastic. It is easier to purchase one that is removable.

Supplies:

4" x 6" Photo Album
Neutral Card Stock
Cream Card Stock
Scissors
2 Eyelets
Jute

1. Remove the front and back covers of the photo album.
2. Reduce the sports photo to approximately 3 1/4" x 4 1/4".
3. Print and trim the photo.
4. Print the child's name and title on cream card stock, leaving enough space for the photo.
5. Trim the cream card stock to approximately 4 1/4" x 5 3/4".
6. Adhere the photo in the center of the cream card stock.
7. Adhere the cream card stock onto neutral card stock leaving a 1/8" border.
8. Insert the photo into the cover sleeve.
9. Cut a piece of card stock for the back cover.
10. Insert eyelets, centered on the sides of the front and back covers.
11. Insert a piece of jute through each eyelet and tie closed.

Congratulations Card (F.)

Supplies:

Light Pink Card Stock
White Card Stock
White Writing Paper
Paper Punch
Wooden Skewer
Scissors
Deckle Edged Scissors

1. Reduce the photo to approximately 2" x 3" and print.
2. Trim and mount the photo on light pink card stock.
3. Using deckle edged scissors, cut the light pink card stock leaving a 1/4" border.
4. Trim both the white writing paper and white card stock to 5 1/2" x 11".
5. Fold both the paper and the card stock in half to measure 5 1/2" x 5 1/2".
6. Place the paper in between the card stock.
7. Punch two holes on the fold line 1" from each side using 2/3 of the punch to create a semi circle.
8. Cut the skewer to approximately 3 1/2" long. Sharpen the cut end to a point and insert through the holes as shown.

40-63B

Headliners & FrameLiners by Combined Provo Craft Artists

Lamp (A.)

Supplies:

- Plain Lampshade
- Unfinished Lamp Base
- Scissors
- Xyron or Spray Mount
- Acrylic Paint
- Mod Podge
- Sponge Brush
- Ribbon or Lace (optional)

1. Paint the lamp base.
2. Print the computer images you want for the base and lampshade.
3. Trim and cut out the images.
4. Use spray mount or Xyron to apply the images to the base and the shade.
5. Use two to three coats of Mod Podge to finish the surface as a sealant.
6. Embellish the base with ribbon.

We're #1 T-Shirt (B.)

Supplies:

- White T-Shirt
- Xerox Iron-On Transfer Paper
- Scissors

1. Choose your image and size it to fit your shirt.
2. Print on transfer paper. (Make sure you indicate on your printer that it is a transfer printed backwards.)
3. Cut around the image.
4. Following the instructions on the packaging, iron the image onto the shirt.

Graduation Page (C.)

Supplies:

- 1 Sheet White Card Stock
- Photo Mounting Squares
- Acid Free Markers
- Colored Card Stock (school colors)
- Acid Free Sheet Protector

1. Print HugWare "The Graduate" in black and white on white card stock.
2. Using markers, color the headliner letters to match your school colors.
3. Mount the graduation announcement on the white card stock.
4. Mount a photo on coordinating card stock and mount on the white card stock.
5. Mount the white card stock onto coordinating card stock.

Plaid Flower Frame (D.)

Supplies:

- Unfinished Picture Frame
- Printed Paper
- Scissors
- Xyron or Spray Mount
- Vellum (optional)
- Mounting Tape
- Paint (optional)
- Ribbon (optional)

Sample Supplies:

- 40-0112 "Spring Break" Scrap Pad

1. Adhere the paper to the frame using Xyron or spray mount. (To soften the look, you can adhere a sheet of vellum, with computer images printed on it, over the paper.)
2. Trim excess paper and cut out the center.
3. Apply the computer images to the frame using mounting tape to add dimension.
4. Paint or embellish the sides with ribbon, whatever your heart desires.

Magnets (E.)

Supplies:

- Magnetic Sheet (12 millimeter matte)
- Scissors

1. Enlarge the images to the size desired.
2. Print the images onto a magnetic sheet.
3. Cut out the images and place on anything metal.

Flower Clock (F.)

Supplies:

- Number Stickers
- 12" x 12" Printed Paper
- Clock with Removable Cover
- Spray Mount or Xyron

Sample Supplies:

- 42-1514 Black "Fat Dot" Alphabitties
- 42-5166 "I'm Sick Plaid" 12" x 12" Paper

1. Take the cover off the clock and trace the shape onto the back of the printed paper for the face of the clock.
2. Use spray mount or Xyron adhesive on the back of the paper, making a slit from the edge to the center to slip around the hands of the clock. You will also need to make a small circle to fit around the hand mechanism.
3. After the paper is positioned on the original face, place computer images in the 12, 3, 6, 9 and center positions. Apply alphabitty numbers as shown.
4. Replace the cover on the clock and there you have it, your own personalized clock created by you!

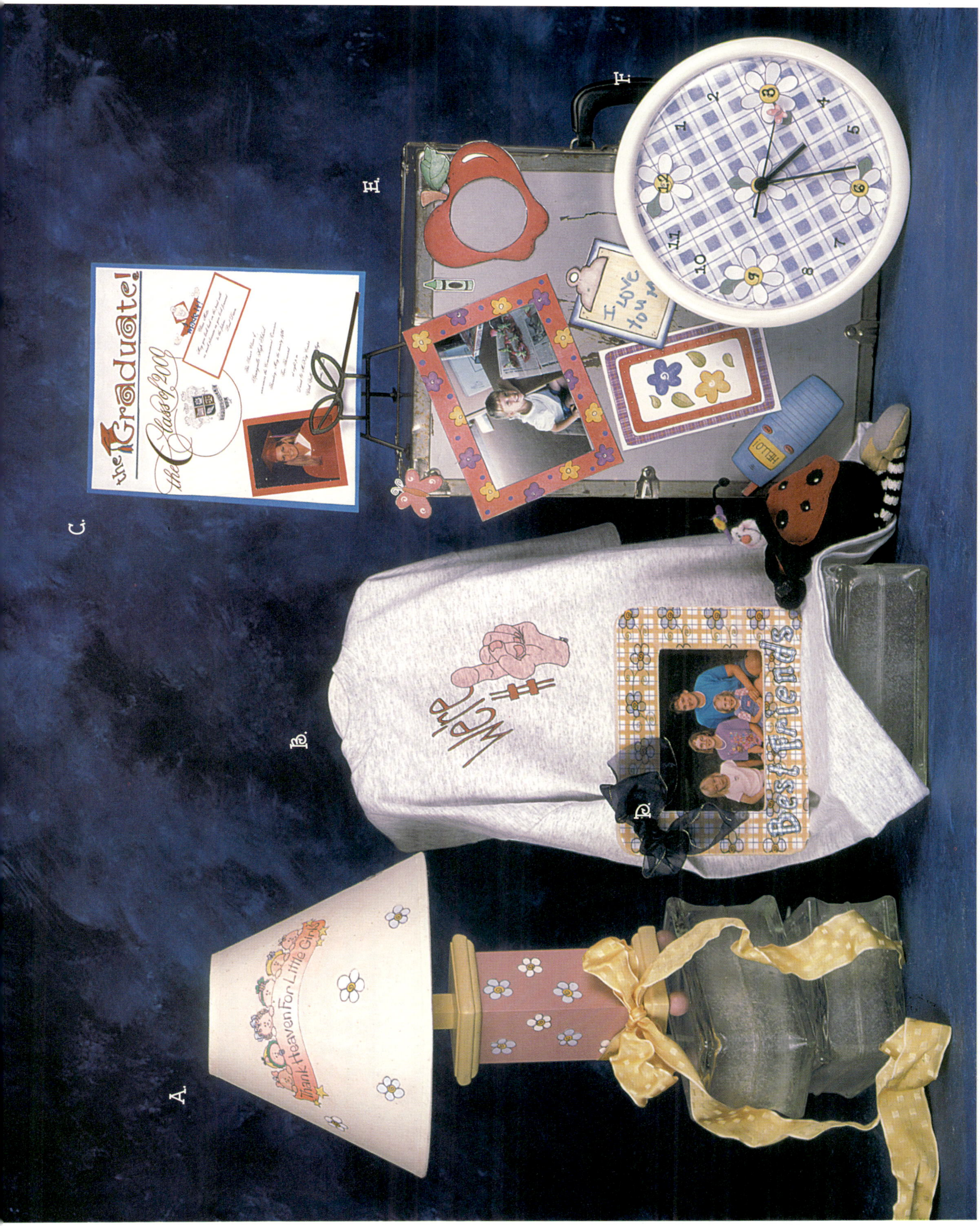
A.
B.
C.
D.
E.
F.
Thank Heaven For Little Girls
the Graduate!
Best Friends

Granny's Doodles by Pat Olson

"Be An Angel" Hang-Up (A.)

Supplies:

- Heavy Watercolor Paper or Card Stock
- Small Scissors
- Clear Acrylic Spray Gloss
- Thin Wire to Hang
- Hole Punch
- Ribbon or Fabric Scrap

1. Print the image on heavy paper.
2. Cut out the image carefully.
3. Spray both sides of the image with several coats of acrylic spray.
4. Punch three holes and hang with twisted wire.
5. Decorate the wire with a piece of fabric or ribbon.

Christmas Ornament or Gift Tag (B.)

Supplies:

- Heavy Card Stock or Watercolor Paper
- Small Scissors
- Clear Acrylic Spray Gloss
- Spray Glitter
- Hole Punch
- Ribbon to Hang

1. Print the images on heavy paper.
2. Carefully cut out the images with small scissors.
3. Spray both sides of the images with several coats of acrylic spray and let dry.
4. Spray with glitter and let dry.
5. Finish with acrylic spray.
6. Punch holes in the top and hang with ribbon.

Bless My Cabin Framed Piece (C.)

Supplies:

- Watercolor Paper
- Rustic 5" x 7" Frame
- Krylon Matte Finish

Palette: Delta Ceramcoat

- Straw
- Red Iron Oxide
- Drizzle Grey
- Pine Green
- Dark Brown
- Flesh Tan

Note: I have hand colored the sample piece, but you could color it on your computer or just use the color design provided.

1. Print the pattern on watercolor paper.
2. Let dry very well. This may take a while as watercolor paper is very porous.
3. Spray with two coats of Krylon Matte Finish.

Hand Paint Method:

1. Use a #2 or #3 round brush to fill in the colors with a watercolor method.
2. Make a wash of the color and just fill in the areas, trying to avoid going over the lines. Don't worry if specks of white show through.
3. Go over areas you want darker, shaded with another coat or a darker wash. Do not fill in an area that butts up against another area until one area is dry or you may have runs.

Stars and Moon	Straw, shaded with Red Iron Oxide
Trees	Pine Green
Tree Trunks	Dark Brown
Cabin	Dark Brown - let dry
Stripes	Flesh Tan
Roof	Red Iron Oxide
Chimney	Drizzle Grey
Door	Red Iron Oxide
Windows	Straw
Grass	Pine Green

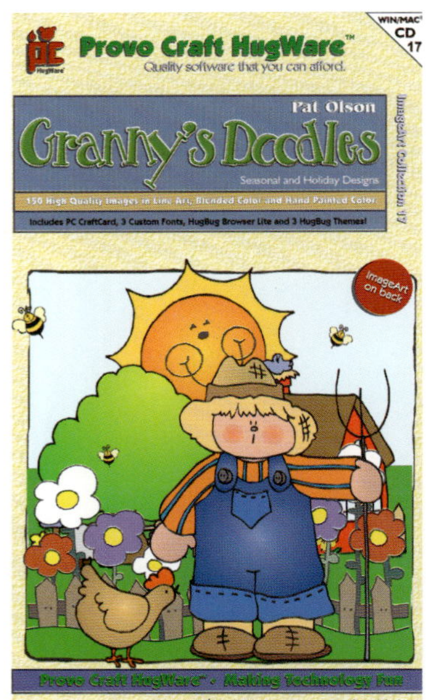

40-6316

A.
Be an Angel
Don't Smoke
B.
B.
B.
C.
Bless My Little cabin
nestled in the pines

Poems for Posterity by Rebecca Hogue

First Easter Scrapbook Page (A.)

Supplies:
- 2 Sheets Scrapbook Paper
- Card Stock
- Photos
- Rub-Ons or Stickers
- Grass Scissors
- Alphabet Stickers

Sample Supplies:
- Coluzzle Nested Hexagon Template (for basket)
- 42-5253 12" x 12" Buttercream "Suede" Paper
- 42-6171 8 1/2" x 11" "Zany Zoo Grass" Paper
- 42-1452 Green "Kids" Alphabet Stickers

1. Choose a font and poem and print on card stock.
2. Mount your photos on scrapbook paper and adhere to the page.
3. Cut out a basket using the Coluzzle Hexagon Template and adhere to the page.
4. Cut out the poem to fit on the basket and adhere to the basket.
5. Using grass scissors, cut the edge of a strip of green paper and adhere to the bottom of the page.
6. Adhere alphabet stickers to the top of the page for a title.
7. Decorate the basket and bottom edge of the page with flower rub-ons or stickers.

Close Knit Family Page (B.)

Supplies:
- Cardboard with stand in back
- Photo
- Scrapbook Paper
- 2 Sheets Coordinating Solid Color Card Stock
- Rub-On Transfers

Sample Supplies:
- 42-6106 8 1/2" x 11" "Natural Pine" Paper
- 41-8514 First Impressions "Spring Borders" Rub-On

1. Cover the cardboard with scrapbook paper.
2. Choose a font and a poem and print on colored card stock.
3. Cut out the poem and mat on coordinating colored card stock.
4. Trim your photo and triple mat.
5. Accent the corners around the photo with rub-ons or stickers.
6. Adhere the poem and photo to the page.

Bath Time Heart Puzzle Magnet (C.)

Supplies:
- Colored Card Stock
- Coluzzle Heart Puzzle
- Foam Core
- Die-Cut Bubbles
- Photo
- Magnet strips

1. Choose a font and print a poem on colored card stock, leaving a space for the puzzle notch.
2. Choose a photo that matches the poem.
3. Position the Coluzzle Heart Puzzle on the photo and cut one side of the heart.
4. Position the other side of the Coluzzle Heart Puzzle on the poem and cut.
5. Position the Coluzzle Heart Puzzle on the foam core and cut out the entire heart.
6. Mount the poem and photo pieces on the foam core.
7. Adhere die-cut bubbles to the edge of the puzzle pieces.
8. Adhere magnet strips to the back of the puzzle pieces.

Happy Grandparent's Day Card (D.)

Supplies:
- Blank White Card or Card Stock
- Vellum
- Scrapbook Paper
- Coordinating Solid Color Card Stock
- Mounting Tape
- Decorative Edged Scissors

Sample Supplies:
- 42-6298 8 1/2" x 11" Heritage Plum "Funky Swirl" Paper

1. Choose a font and print a greeting on vellum.
2. Print a poem and your closing remarks on white card stock.
3. Cover the outside of the card with scrapbook paper.
4. Cut out the vellum greeting and adhere to the front cover.
5. Make a border with coordinating solid color card stock using decorative edged scissors and adhere around the vellum greeting.
6. Cut out the poem and closing remarks and mount on solid color card stock. Adhere to the inside of the card.

Personalized Calendar (E.)

Supplies:
- Scrapbook Paper
- Solid Color Card Stock
- Paper Punches
- Scissors or Paper Cutter
- Adhesive

Sample Supplies:
- Filigree Heart Die-Cuts by Accu-Cut
- Swirl Border Punch by All Night Media
- "February" die-cut by Katee's Kut Ups
- 42-6312 8 1/2" x 11" Pomegranate "Polka-Dot" Paper
- 42-6313 8 1/2" x 11" Pomegranate "Suede" Paper
- 42-6316 8 1/2" x 11" Pomegranate "Basic Check" Paper
- Black Card Stock

1. Print out the calendar pages on heavy white paper.
2. Decorate each month with appropriate photos, matching holidays or special occasions for the month.
3. Print a poem appropriate for each month.
4. Mount the photos and poems on scrapbook paper and card stock.
5. Using a paper punch, decorate the borders.

The Cutting Edge by Anne Fetzer

"Let it Grow" Picture Frame (A.)

Supplies:

- Large Frame with Glass
- Mounting Tape
- Crimper
- 5 sheets PC Soft Watercolor Paper in 5 different colors

1. Open "Let it Grow" black and white outline image.
2. Print a copy on each of the 5 sheets of paper.
3. Cut pieces out following pattern.
4. Crimp paper pieces and layer using mounting tape.
5. Frame and hang.

Boxes and Bags (B.)

Supplies:

- Bag or Cardboard Box (any size or shape)
- Card Stock or White Paper
- Spray Adhesive
- Regular Sized Scissors
- Small Detailed Scissors

1. Choose an image and size it to fit the box or bag.
2. Print the image on card stock or white paper.
3. Cut out the image using small scissors for cutting around the details.
4. Using spray adhesive, mount the image to the lid of the box or front of the bag. (To help center the image, make markings on the lid or bag.)

Cards (C.)

Supplies:

- Blank Card or Card Stock (cut and folded)
- Card Stock or White Paper
- Regular Sized Scissors
- Small Detail Scissors
- Spray Adhesive

1. Choose an image and size it to fit the card.
2. Print the image on card stock or white paper.
3. Cut out the image using small scissors to cut around the details.
4. Using spray adhesive, mount the image on the front of the card. (To help center the image, make markings on the front of the card.)

Notebook (D.)

Supplies:

- Notebook with Image Cut-Out
- White Paper
- Scissors
- Spray Adhesive

1. Choose an image and size it to fit the notebook cut-out.
2. Print the image on white paper.
3. Cut out the image to fit in the notebook cut-out.
4. Using spray adhesive, mount the image in the cut-out.

40-6318

A.
LET IT GROW
B.
B.
Sunflower
C.
Sunflower
B.
C.
B.
D.
B.

Noah, Moses & Friends by Deena Rutter

Starlight Pillow (A.)

Supplies:

- Transfer Iron-On Paper
- Heat and Bond
- Polyester Stuffing
- Embroidery Floss
- 7" x 10" Muslin (tea-dyed)
- 12" x 12" Muslin (for back of pillow)
- 12" x 12" Fabric (for front of pillow)
- 40-6319 Noah, Moses and Friends CD
- Lucky Stars Border

1. Select and import the border you would like to use. (I started with a black and white image of the Lucky Stars border and added the colors that accented the fabric I wanted to use.)
2. Flip the image horizontally. Print onto transfer iron-on paper.
3. Follow the instructions on how to use this paper and iron the image onto the fabric. (I used tea-dyed muslin.)
4. Apply "heat and bond" to the back of the tea-dyed muslin.
5. With a light pencil, in the inside square of the border write: Star Light, Star Bright, Don't Forget to Pray Tonight.
6. Stitch over the penciled letters with embroidery floss.
7. Iron the tea-dyed fabric to the center of the fabric to be used for the front of the pillow.
8. Stitch around the square image with embroidery floss.
9. Sew the pillow together, leaving an opening for stuffing.
10. Turn right side out, lightly stuff and sew closed. Using embroidery floss, stitch around the sides of the pillow.

Noah's Ark Flannel Board (B.)

Supplies:

- White Paper
- Scissors
- Laminate
- Sticky Back Velcro

1. Print the images on white paper.
2. Cut out the images, leaving a small white border.
3. Laminate all of the images.
4. Adhere Velcro to back of the images.

Noah's Ark Bag (C.)

Supplies:

- White Canvas Bag
- Transfer Iron-On Paper
- Red Embroidery Floss
- Buttons

1. Enlarge the image to fit your bag and print on transfer iron-on paper.
2. Follow the instructions on how to use this paper and iron the image onto your bag.
3. Sew a running stitch around the top of the bag using embroidery floss.
4. Sew buttons onto the image.

Quiet Book (D.)

1. Select and import each quiet book page into a document.
2. If you have a program that will let you type on your image, add your child's name to the quiet book title.
3. Resize the image to fit 7 1/2" x 8" quiet book pages.
4. Print onto the "book template".
5. To bind the book, staple the front cover to the quiet book pages.
6. Use a laminate for the front cover and binding tape to bind the book together.
7. Enjoy your quiet time while your children enjoy their very own quiet book.

Say Your Prayers (E.)

Supplies:

- 2 Coordinating Colored Card Stock
- White High Quality Paper
- Scissors
- Hole Punch
- Ribbon or Rope

1. Choose a border and picture (feminine or masculine) and print a color copy on white paper or color it yourself.
2. Cut out the picture, leaving a small white border.
3. Cut the colored card stock for matting the picture, as shown.
4. Adhere the picture to the card stock, leaving a larger border at the top.
5. Punch two holes at the top.
6. Thread the holes with rope or ribbon and tie.
7. Hang on the bedpost, dresser knob, door knob or wall.

E.

40-6319